Published by
Vegan Publishers
Danvers, MA
www.veganpublishers.com
Orders (978) 829-2525
contact@veganpublishers.com

Art by Sabrina Bedford
Recipes by Ellie Bedford

ISBN: 978-1-940184-22-7
Library of Congress Control Number: 2014909638

Second Edition, printed and bound in the UK, 2015

Vegan Publishers™

How to Eat a Rainbow
Magical Raw Vegan Recipes for Kids!

Recipes by Ellie Bedford
Illustrations by Sabrina Bedford

For Sofia and Dorrie, the cutest fairies we know!

 Vegan Publishers™

Table of Contents

A note about measurements:
These recipes were tested in UK cups. The difference between UK and US cups is small and should not affect the final outcome.

Introduction

Our Fairy Important Secret!

Have you ever wondered where we fairies get our sparkle? Why we're so happy?

Well, I'm going to let you in on a little secret: the secret is our food! To keep our wings strong and give us energy for our important fairy duties, we eat a rainbow every day. We grow all our food in our magical fairy garden, which means our recipes are super fresh and bursting with vitamins and minerals.

This book is a collection of our very best fairy recipes of raw food that are tasty and fun to make. A raw food is a vegetable, fruit, nut or seed that has not been heated too much. These foods are full of intact enzymes and are living foods, the way nature intended. They help children grow big and strong! Each recipe needs only what's grown in our fairy garden and nothing else! These recipes work well at snack, dessert and breakfast times, and they are designed to be easily added to anyone's diet. These foods can add an extra boost of energy and get everyone excited about healthy eating.

Our recipes have been taste tested and approved by our own little fairies. Eating these vegetables, fruits, nuts and other superfoods every day can be difficult, but with a little creativity, fun and fairy magic, everyone can grow up learning about the importance of eating well and enjoying nature's goodness.

After trying all the recipes, you'll eat just like a real fairy! You might need some help, so make sure you have a grown-up with you while trying a recipe!

Once you've mastered our fairy skills, you'll find a special certificate at the end of the book just for you!

Snacks
&
Sides

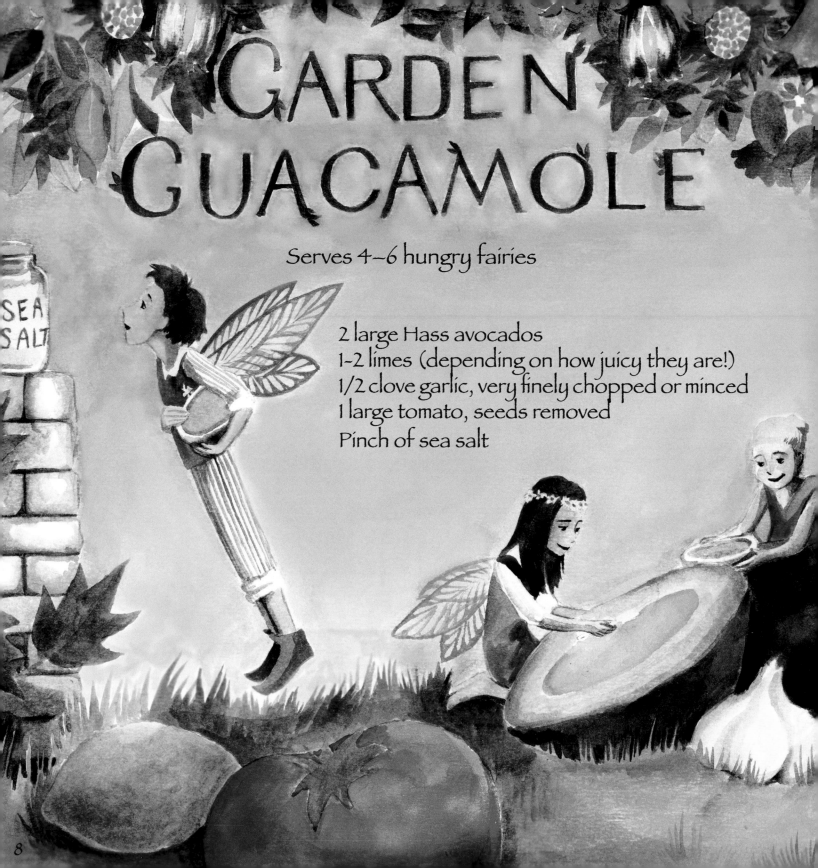

GARDEN GUACAMOLE

Serves 4–6 hungry fairies

2 large Hass avocados
1-2 limes (depending on how juicy they are!)
1/2 clove garlic, very finely chopped or minced
1 large tomato, seeds removed
Pinch of sea salt

SEA SALT

Fairy fact! Avocados are full of good fats, which keep our skin healthy and soft!

We fairies love guacamole! This is a perfect summer dish.

Take a spoon and scoop the avocado out of its skin; then, mash it up slightly in a pestle and mortar. Slice the tomato very finely and add this to the avocado along with the lime juice, garlic and salt. Now for the fun bit! Pound it until it's the texture you like. We think it's more tasty lumpy! If you don't have a pestle and mortar, you can mash it with a fork.

Serve with crunchy crudités and organic tortilla chips! We love colourful red peppers, celery, carrot and cucumber.

Flower Petal Salad

Serves 4 fairies as a side

Flower petals make for a beautiful and tasty fairy salad. Since some flowers can make us feel poorly, be sure to check with a grown-up who can tell if you have the right ones and that they are free from any nasty chemicals! Quite often, you can buy edible flowers in your local supermarket, so keep an eye out for those.

3 cups pea shoots
1 cup sunflower seed sprouts
1 cup baby spinach
2 handfuls of seasonal, edible flower petals. Try a mix or one of the following:

Borage flowers
Dandelion petals
Courgette (zucchini) flower petals
Rose petals
English marigold petals

Arrange the salad leaves, seed sprouts and flower petals on a plate and dress them with olive oil and fresh lemon juice.

Hidden Corn Valley Salsa

Serves 4 fairies as a side

This fresh corn salsa is a great side dish. Enjoy it with your favourite dinner, or make it the star of a whole-grain wrap for a speedy snack!

For the dressing:
1 Tbsp brown rice syrup
1 Tbsp apple cider vinegar
1 Tbsp flax seed oil
1/4 tsp each of sea salt and black pepper

For the salsa:
2 organic ears of corn
1 red bell pepper
2-3 large tomatoes
1/2 red onion
1 handful of fresh coriander (cilantro) or parsley, roughly torn

Ask an adult to slice the corn kernels carefully from the cob and to help you finely dice the onion, tomatoes and bell pepper. Add these to a mixing bowl with the herbs and mix lightly.

Next, make your dressing. Put all of the dressing ingredients into a jar and shake, shake, shake! Pour this dressing over the vegetables and mix well to coat. Now it's ready to go!

SUNFLOWER POWER
Seed Paté

Serves 8–10 little fairies

The sunshine energy from the bright yellow sunflower is brought to life in this flower power paté.

Pop all your ingredients into your food processor and whiz it together until well blended. You can make the paté very smooth, or you can keep it with some texture—whatever you prefer!

Sunflower Seeds

Pour and scrape it out into a little loaf tin or dish and let it cool in the fridge for an hour to make it easier to spread.

Magic tip! This tastes fabulous with crudités, on brown rice cakes or on your favourite crackers!

2 cups sunflower seeds, soaked overnight and drained
10 sun-blushed tomatoes
10 olives in oil and herbs, drained (We love Kalamata olives.)
2 tsp tamari
1 tsp fresh or dried herbs (Try Oregano or Herbes de Provence.)
3 Tbsp extra virgin olive oil
1 clove garlic, grated
Juice of 1 lemon
Zest of 1/2 lemon
Sea salt and pepper to taste

15

Purple Haystack Salad

Makes 4 stacks

1 cup grated carrot
1 cup grated beetroot
1 pink grapefruit, peeled and segmented
1 small pinch of pink Himalayan salt
1 Tbsp lemon juice
1 Tbsp fresh basil or mint, finely shredded
1 tsp coconut palm sugar

Little stacks of brightly coloured vegetables make your dinner plate come alive!

Mix everything together well and pile onto your plates in little haystacks.

ANCIENT PINEWOOD PESTO

Makes enough for 4–6 fairies

The best-kept secret of our pinewoods are these silky little seeds, which are found in the trees. This pesto tastes great on almost anything; try it over whole-grain pasta, baked potatoes, zucchini noodles or quinoa.

Fairy fact! Hemp seeds are a fantastic source of omega-3s, which are good for our brain, heart and eye health, and they are full of protein too!

1 small bunch of basil
1 small bunch of parsley
1-2 cloves of garlic, crushed
1/2 cup pine nuts
1/2 cup shelled hemp seeds
1/4 cup extra virgin olive oil
Sea salt to taste
Zest and juice of one lemon

Blend everything together in a mini chopper or processor, or crush together in a pestle and mortar. You can make this as smooth or chunky as you like.

Vegetable Kebabs

Makes 8 kebabs

These pretty kebabs are so colourful and easy to make; they would be great at any little fairy's birthday party!

For the "cheesy" sauce:
2 cups cashews, soaked overnight and drained
2 cups macadamia nuts, soaked overnight and drained
Juice of one large lemon
1/4 tsp fine sea salt
1/4 tsp ground paprika
1 tsp liquid coconut aminos (optional)
Small clove of garlic, chopped fine

Put all of the "cheesy" sauce ingredients into a food processor and process until the cheese sauce looks smooth and creamy. You can add a little filtered water if you think the cheese sauce is too thick!

For the kebabs:
16 cherry tomatoes
1 yellow bell pepper, cut into 2 1/2-cm (1-inch) chunks
1 green bell pepper, cut into 2 1/2-cm (1-inch) chunks
8 small pink radishes
1 small cucumber, sliced in half lengthways and diced into 1-cm thick "half-moon" chunks
16 button mushrooms, wiped over with a damp cloth

Using eight bamboo skewers, divide the vegetables out evenly and put each group on one of the skewers! Make sure you get a good mix of vegetables on each one, so that they are super colourful. Be careful, as the skewers are sharp. Place them on a large plate while you make the cheese sauce.

Smoothies
&
Elixirs

Pink Lemonade

Makes 4–6 glasses

Perfect for an afternoon tea party, this zingy drink is sure to delight all your friends.

4 lemons
1 cup strawberries, stalks removed
3 cups diced watermelon
6 cups filtered water

Juice the lemons with a lemon juicer and
be careful not to get any seeds in the juice!

Blend everything together with an immersion or
jug blender and enjoy straightaway.

Ruby Punch

Serves 4 little or 2 big fairies

2 apples
4 large carrots
1 large beetroot
1/2 lemon

This pretty juice gets its bright colour from both fruit and vegetables and is naturally sweet.

Wash all the fruit and vegetables in filtered water to make sure we don't catch any of our little bug friends! Then core the apple and cut it into quarters, keeping the skin on.

Fairy fact! Carrots belong to a group of vegetables called root vegetables. These vegetables are special because they grow underground. Carrots are full of vitamin A and are great for our eyes!

Scrape the carrots to remove any dirt and slice them in half lengthwise. Peel and quarter the beetroot. Slice the 1/2 lemon in two. You can keep the skin on.

Juice the carrots first in your juicer. Keep the carrot pulp; you might be able to use it later! Next, juice the remainder of the ingredients to make a beautiful, rich and red colour. Stir and serve straightaway!

Green Goblin Smoothie

Serves 1 fairy

1 banana
1/4 cup fresh or frozen berries
2-3 romaine lettuce leaves
1 cup coconut water or nut milk
1/2 tsp spirulina (optional)

Magic tip! Have fun with this recipe—change up the fruit and the greens: mango makes a delicious, creamy smoothie, and parsley is refreshing and super good for you!

This makes a delicious breakfast or snack, and you won't believe the colour!

Blend everything together to make a super green drink that will amaze all your friends!

BERRY BLUE SMOOTHIE

Serves 2 fairies, perfect to share

1 cup blueberries or purple grapes
2 Tbsp acai or blackcurrant powder
(Fresh blackberries are also good.)
800 ml (27 fl oz) of nut or seed milk
1-2 Tbsp maple syrup (optional)
2 semi-frozen bananas
1/2 avocado
Seeds of one vanilla pod

Magic tip! Both the banana and the avocado give this smoothie a delicious creaminess. You can use all avocados or all bananas if you prefer and adjust the amount of syrup to taste!

The deep, rich colours in this smoothie help us stay well and active in the winter.

For foods rich in antioxidants, look out for pretty blue and purple foods!

Blend everything together until smooth and creamy.

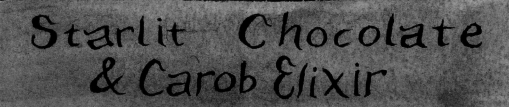

Starlit Chocolate & Carob Elixir

Serves 4 very little fairies or 2 big fairies

We cannot imagine a better drink to enjoy on a starry winter's night than our magical chocolate elixir. It's thick, creamy and sweet and will warm you all the way to the tips of your toes! The carob adds a touch of sweetness and has no caffeine, which makes it gentler than using cacao alone.

600 ml (20 fl oz) of your favourite non-dairy milk
2-3 Tbsp coconut palm sugar or maple syrup
1/2 tsp rose hip powder or dried lavender
2 heaped tsp raw cacao or cocoa powder
1 tsp sugar-free vanilla extract
2 heaped tsp raw carob powder
1 Tbsp purple corn powder
1 tsp tapioca flour
4 Tbsp filtered water
1 tsp ground cinnamon
1/4 tsp ground allspice

Fairy fact! Did you know that the beautiful orangey-red rose hips are full of vitamin C? Rose hip powder is perfect for helping us stay healthy through the winter, but if you can't find it this drink will still be warming and delicious!

Make a paste with the cacao, purple corn, rose hip powder, tapioca flour and the water, and mix until smooth and lump free. Add to a saucepan along with the rest of the ingredients, bring to a medium heat and stir with a whisk for around 6 minutes until thick and creamy, taking care not to bring to a boil.

33

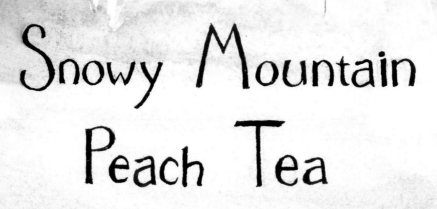

Snowy Mountain Peach Tea

Serves 2 fairies

3 ripe peaches or nectarines, pitted and chopped
1 Tbsp fresh lemon juice
2 pitted Medjool dates, chopped
1 1/2 cups cooled rooibos tea
1 cup ice

Frosty and sweet, this is a super refreshing drink for sharing on a hot summer's day.

Magic tip! Have fun and experiment with this recipe using different fruit and fruit tea combinations. Berry tea with a cup of fresh blueberries is also tasty.

TEA

Blend everything together in a blender. We like to serve this tea in tall glasses with a straw.

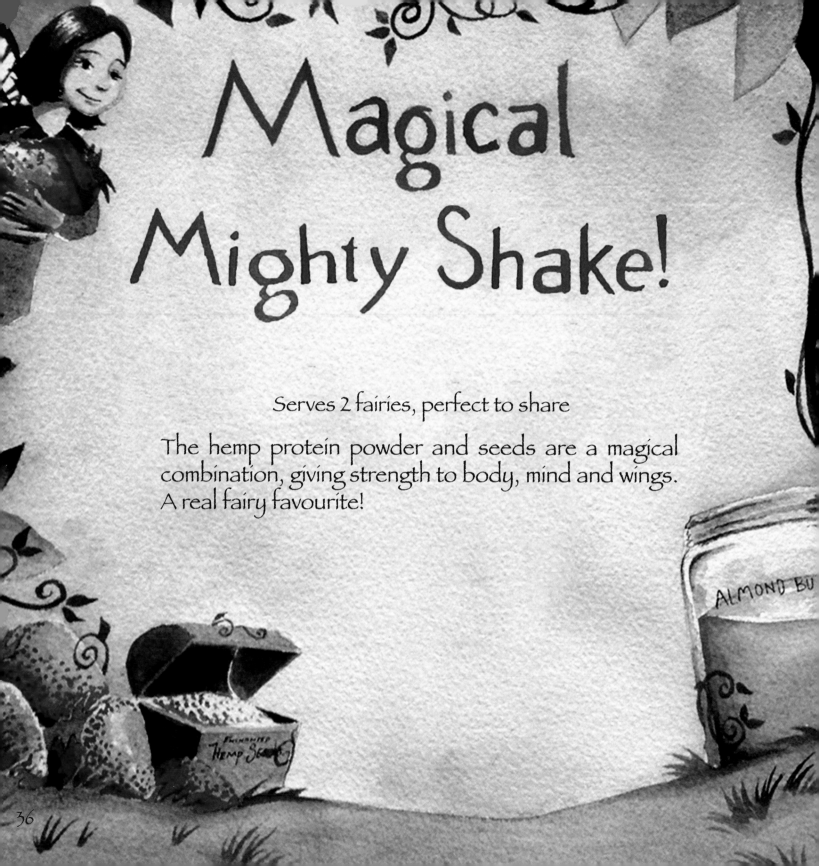

Magical Mighty Shake!

Serves 2 fairies, perfect to share

The hemp protein powder and seeds are a magical combination, giving strength to body, mind and wings. A real fairy favourite!

4 pitted dates, soaked and drained, or 1 Tbsp brown rice syrup
2 Tbsp of hemp/rice protein powder (or 1/4 cup hemp seeds)
400 ml (14 fl oz) hemp or non-dairy milk of choice
1 banana (optional, it works great without too)
2 Tbsp almond butter
12-14 frozen strawberries
1 Tbsp hemp seeds
Seeds of one vanilla pod or 1/2 tsp vanilla powder

Add everything to a blender and blitz until smooth and creamy. Get ready for feelings of superpower!

Treats
&
Sweets

Dreamy Mousse

Serves 2–4 fairies

Can you guess the secret ingredient in this dessert? Shhh, it's avocado! That is what gives it the delicious creaminess and texture just like chocolate pudding.

2 large ripe avocados (Hass are good.)
6 pitted, dried prunes
1 Tbsp filtered water
2 Tbsp raw cocoa, cacao or carob powder
3 Tbsp maple syrup
Seeds of 1/2 vanilla pod

Remove the seeds from the vanilla pod by cutting it in half and scraping them out with a spoon—you may need help with this part.

Sneak Peak Recipe from How to Eat a Rainbow:
Magical Raw Vegan Recipes for Kids!
Recipes by Ellie Bedford
Illustrations by Sabrina Bedford

Add the seeds to the processor with the prunes,
avocado, maple syrup and cacao powder and
process until creamy. Refrigerate for an hour to
set before enjoying.

Rainbow Flan

Serves 6–8 fairies

A rainbow on a plate! The fruit tastes delicious with the rich chocolate topping, and you can decorate the fruit in any pattern you like.

Blitz the dates until they are nice and small in your food processor. Then add in all the rest of the ingredients. Blitz again, until the mixture looks like fine breadcrumbs. Tip the mixture out into a large flan case and press flat with the back of a spoon.

To make smaller flans, just put the cutter on a plate, spoon 2 Tbsps of mixture into each one, press flat and then remove the cutter, leaving a little crust.

To make the base:
1 Tbsp of coconut oil, melted
125 g (4 1/2 oz) pitted dates
50g (2 oz) desiccated coconut
50g (20 oz) ground almonds
1/4 tsp cinnamon
Pinch of sea salt

ALMO

DATE

Magic tip! To keep your fruit from turning brown, toss it in a little lemon juice.

To make the chocolate topping:
200g (7 oz) cashew nuts
2 Tbsp melted coconut oil
1 Tbsp melted cacao butter
140 ml (5 fl oz) of filtered water
2-3 Tbsp maple syrup
3 Tbsp raw cacao powder
Pinch of fine sea salt
The seeds of one vanilla pod

Put all the ingredients into a food processor and blend until perfectly creamy and smooth. You may need to stop the food processor a few times to scrape down the sides of the bowl.

To make the flan:
Spread the chocolate filling over the base of your flan(s). Make the topping as thick as you like! Decorate with fresh fruit of your choice. We fairies love raspberries, bananas, kiwis and cape gooseberries, but you can use any kind you like--the more colourful the better. Remember, you're making a rainbow!

Pop it in the fridge for 30 minutes to 1 hour to firm up before serving.

PB&J
FOREST TWIGS

Makes 4 "twigs"

These taste just like a peanut butter and jam sandwich, only they are delicate and light!

Allow one half to one "twig" as a snack.

NUT BUTTER

4 sticks celery, well washed
4-5 Tbsp almond or cashew butter
3/4 cup of dehydrated or dried strawberries

Fill the celery with the nut butter and top with the dehydrated strawberries: delicious and pretty!

45

Jewelled Chia Seed Pudding

Serves 4–6 fairies

An amazingly quick treat to make, it can be made up before you go to sleep and will be ready for a super speedy breakfast in the morning.

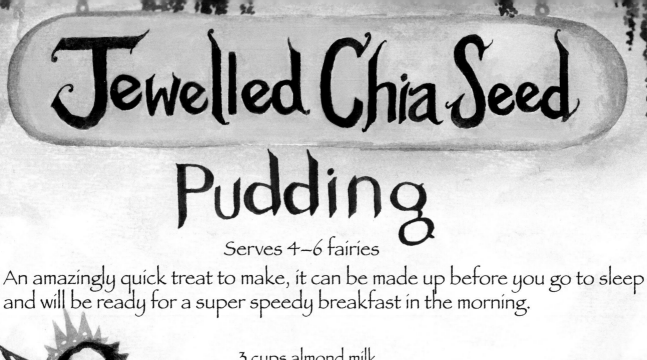

3 cups almond milk
2 tsp sugar and alcohol-free vanilla extract, or the seeds of one vanilla pod
1/2 cup chia seeds
1 tsp cinnamon
1/2 cup goji berries
Maple syrup for drizzling
Zest of 1/2 lemon
Seeds of one pomegranate

Fairy fact! Chia seeds may be tiny, but they're packed with omega-3 fatty acids, which are important for a healthy heart. They are a super protein food that gives us the energy we need to be busy all day!

The goji berries and pomegranate seeds in this creamy pudding sparkle like real fairy jewels.

Add the chia, vanilla, cinnamon and milk to a 1-litre (1-quart) mason jar. Pop the lid on and shake away! Have a fun little shaky dance around the kitchen to make sure it is well mixed. Pop it in the fridge before you go to bed and wait for the magic to happen.

When you wake up, check your breakfast. It will have turned into a thick and creamy custardy pudding! Pour into bowls and top each portion with the pomegranate, goji berries, lemon zest and a drizzle of maple syrup. Enjoy!

Apple Moon Pie

Makes 1 pie

This delicious pie has a lot of ingredients, but it is worth the extra effort. Perfect for a fairy gathering or party!

For the walnut crust:
1/2 cup walnuts
1/2 cup ground almonds
1/2 cup desiccated coconut
10 Medjool dates, pitted
1 Tbsp coconut oil
Pinch of pink Himalayan salt

Blitz together all of the ingredients, in a food processor, until the mixture starts to stick together a little. Ask an adult to help with this part.

Tip the mixture into a 20-cm (8-inch) loose-bottomed pie dish. Press the mixture into the dish to line the bottom and sides with a delicious crust. You can then pop this in the fridge to firm up while you make the filling.

For the apple pie filling:
4 medium-sized apples, cores removed
1 Tbsp maple or brown rice syrup
1-2 tsp ground cinnamon
1/4 tsp ground allspice
2 large pears (They need to be very ripe and juicy!)
Juice of 1/2 lemon
Pinch of fine pink Himalayan salt

Quarter each of the apples and then slice the quarters into thin half-moon-shaped slices. Pop these into a bowl and coat them well with the lemon juice to stop them from turning brown.

Ask a fairy grown-up helper to help peel and core the pears and put them in a mini chopper or food processor. Add the maple or rice syrup, salt and spices and puree them. You are looking to achieve as smooth a puree as possible.

Tip this mix into the apples and stir to coat really well. Tip most of this mixture into your prepared piecrust and press down well. With the remaining apple, arrange the slices in a circular pattern on the top to make it look extra special! Chill for 30 minutes and it's ready to go!

Peppermint Cream Clouds

Makes around 20 little clouds

These little peppermint creams are totally dreamy and melt in your mouth just like a little fluffy cloud!

1/2 cup of creamed coconut*, grated
1 Tbsp virgin coconut oil
1 Tbsp coconut cream
2 Tbsp maple, agave or rice syrup
1 1/2 tsp peppermint extract
2 Tbsp lucuma powder, plus extra for dusting
40g (1 1/2 oz) of your favourite raw chocolate

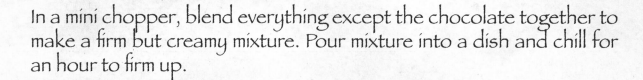

In a mini chopper, blend everything except the chocolate together to make a firm but creamy mixture. Pour mixture into a dish and chill for an hour to firm up.

Generously dust a work surface with lucuma powder and tip out the chilled mixture; roll the mixture into a ball of dough, adding a little more lucuma if it becomes very sticky.

Press the mixture flat with your hands to about 1/2-cm (1/8-inch) thick. Cut out small cloud shapes or rounds around 3 1/2 cm (1 1/2 inch) in diameter.

Place the clouds onto a plate to chill a little while you gently melt the raw chocolate. To melt it, break the chocolate up into pieces in a bowl and stand the bowl in very hot water, stirring the chocolate until melted. Drizzle the melted chocolate over the peppermint creams and chill for a further 15 minutes until set.

*You can find blocks of creamed coconut in specialist stores or online.

CHOCOLATE BROWNIES

Makes about 20 tasty bites

These brownies take no time at all to whiz up and make the perfect handy treat when we're out and about on our fairy duties! Pop one of these into your bag and you'll have a healthy snack wherever you go.

200 g (7 oz) cashew nuts
10 Medjool dates, pitted and roughly chopped
10 soft unsulphured apricots
2 Tbsp raw cacao, cocoa or carob powder
1 Tbsp lucuma powder
2-4 drops food-grade orange oil (optional)
Pinch of pink Himalayan salt or fine sea salt

In a food processor, blitz the cashews until they are as fine as you can get them. Loosen the mix a little from the bottom and then add the remainder of the filling ingredients.

Blitz again until the mixture starts to come together as a ball of dough. Press the dough well into a 20 x 15-cm (8 x 6-inch) Pyrex brownie pan and put it in the fridge to chill for half an hour.

When it's chilled, cut the brownie into even-sized squares. When you're ready to go out on an adventure, wrap a brownie square in a piece of grease-proof paper and it's ready to take!

Magic tip! This mixture tastes great as cake pops! Simply roll the mix into balls, pop them on sticks and coat them with your favourite raw chocolate!

53

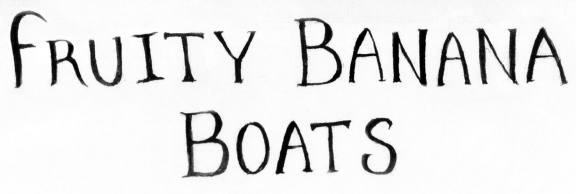

FRUITY BANANA BOATS

Makes 4 boats

This is a pretty impressive looking dessert: golden banana boats filled with fruity jewels, just like the boats floating down our magical rivers.

For the boats:
4 bananas
1/2 cup blueberries
1/2 cup raspberries
1/2 cup green grapes, halved

Peel the bananas and slice in half lengthwise, but do not cut all the way to the bottom. You just want a split in the banana that can be filled with delicious fruits. Divide the blueberries, raspberries and grapes between the boats and finish with a dollop of the cashew cream and a drizzle of the strawberry sauce.

For the cashew cream:
1 cup cashew nuts, soaked overnight
1 Tbsp lemon juice
2 Tbsp brown rice syrup
1/2 cup filtered water
Seeds of 1/2 a vanilla pod

Drain the cashews and add them to a blender or food processor. Put the other ingredients in and blend until smooth and creamy.

For the strawberry sauce:
2 cups strawberries
2 Tbsp chia seeds

Blend them together with a stick blender and set aside for 20–30 minutes. The sauce will thicken into a delicious, ruby-red jam!`

Magic tip! If you haven't got time to soak your cashews, try this with almond or coconut yoghurt. It tastes just as delicious!

Glossary!

Acai and Blackcurrant Powder
Both of these powders contain magical antioxidants thanks to their beautiful, deep, purple colours.

Brown Rice Syrup
A gentle sweetener that is often used in raw recipes, brown rice syrup has a mild and malty taste and is a fairy favourite!

Cacao Powder (raw)
Like cocoa powder, only it hasn't been roasted! You can use both kinds in your recipes, depending on which you prefer.

Carob Powder
This is great if you want a lovely mixture of chocolate and toffee flavours in dishes. Because it contains no caffeine, it is a great alternative to chocolate for children.

Coconut Palm Sugar
Coconut palm sugar is not raw, but it's often used in raw foods because it's minimally processed and mineral rich and has a low GI compared to other sweeteners. It also tastes great!

Dates
Sticky and sweet, dates taste like toffee and are great in all kinds of desserts.

Extra Virgin Olive Oil
This has a tasty, peppery flavour and is delicious in dips and spreads.

Flaxseed (Linseed)
This amazing omega-3 packed seed needs to be ground to get the full benefits. You can buy it already ground or grind it yourself. Be sure to store it in the fridge to keep it fresh.

Goji Berries
These are tasty little red berries that are easy to find dried. They are full of vitamin C and contain all essential amino acids—great for vegan fairies!

Hemp Seeds
This seed is full of healthy omega fats and has a very mild and creamy taste. It's great sprinkled on anything and delicious when made into a milk.

Lucuma
A nutrient-dense fruit powder, which adds a subtle, sweet flavour to dishes!

Maple Syrup
Although maple syrup is not raw, it still contains important vitamins and minerals, unlike refined cane sugar. It has a delicious, sweet, smoky flavour that works really well in desserts.

Purple Corn Powder
A great gluten-free thickener for sauces and smoothies, it has a mild and smooth taste and is packed full of nutrients.

Spirulina
These amazing green algae have high protein content and are full of minerals. They also blend really well into smoothies to give them a healthy boost.

Sunflower Seeds
Sweet little seeds with a mild taste and full of vitamin E—we fairies add them to all sorts of dishes, from breakfast muesli to spreads, and as crunchy toppings.

Virgin Coconut Oil
This oil is thick and creamy and is solid at room temperature. This is really useful for setting up raw desserts or for creating a smoother texture to dishes.

Fairy Tools!

Blender (Jug or Stick)
A great tool to blend up whole fruits and greens to make delicious smoothies.

Chopping Board
To protect our kitchen tops and make tidying away a breeze.

Food Processor/Mini Chopper
We use this to blend nuts together to make creamy toppings, as well as magically turning dried fruits to brownies and other yummy treats. Be careful not to touch the sharp blades!

Juicer
Turns whole fruits and vegetables into colorful juices. This really does work like magic!

Knife
We have to be very careful with knives, and it's best that a grown-up helps with the cutting; but without them we'd be quite stuck!

Lemon Juicer
Helps squeeze all the goodness out of lemons and oranges whilst keeping those seeds out of our food.

Melon Scoop
An easy way for us to get perfect portions of melon and other fruits, without needing to use a knife.

Pestle and Mortar
A great tool that little fairies can use all by themselves. We use it for blending and mixing just like you would a magic cauldron!

Scales and Cup Measurements
For measuring the perfect quantities of ingredients to create a dish fit for a fairy!

Skewers
Great for threading fruits and veggies together to make tasty kebabs.

Spatula
A special scraping tool that helps us use every last bit of our creations.

Wand (optional)
To add that extra sparkle!

When making fairy recipes, it's good to know these helpful words. These gadgets save lots of time and mess in the kitchen and are also fun to use!

Certificate
for Fairy Cookery

PRESENTED TO

_____

Acknowledgments

Thank you so much to all our amazing family and friends for your support; this wouldn't have been possible without you! Thank you to all our campaign supporters who donated and shared our campaign and everybody involved behind the scenes who helped make it such a success. And a very big thank you to Vegan Publishers for believing in fairies!

INDEX

About the author:

Ellie Bedford is a home educating mum of two little girls, an award winning food blogger, and a Raw and Wholefood Consultant in Oxfordshire, England.

Ellie has written recipes and articles both online and for magazine publications and speaks at health festivals and events around the UK. Her passion for family health takes her to schools and youth organisations, where she shares the fun and ease of raw foods with children, believing that reaching children early encourages a healthy relationship with food.

About the illustrator:

Sabrina Bedford, Ellie's sister-in-law, is an artist, writer and illustrator currently living in California.

She hosts arts and crafts workshops around the world with children and adults, promoting health and wellbeing through creative expression.

She is always illustrating, painting and drawing both independently and through collaborations. Sabrina loves book-making and narrative art. She seeks to tell compelling and inspiring stories in her work.

Fairy Notes!